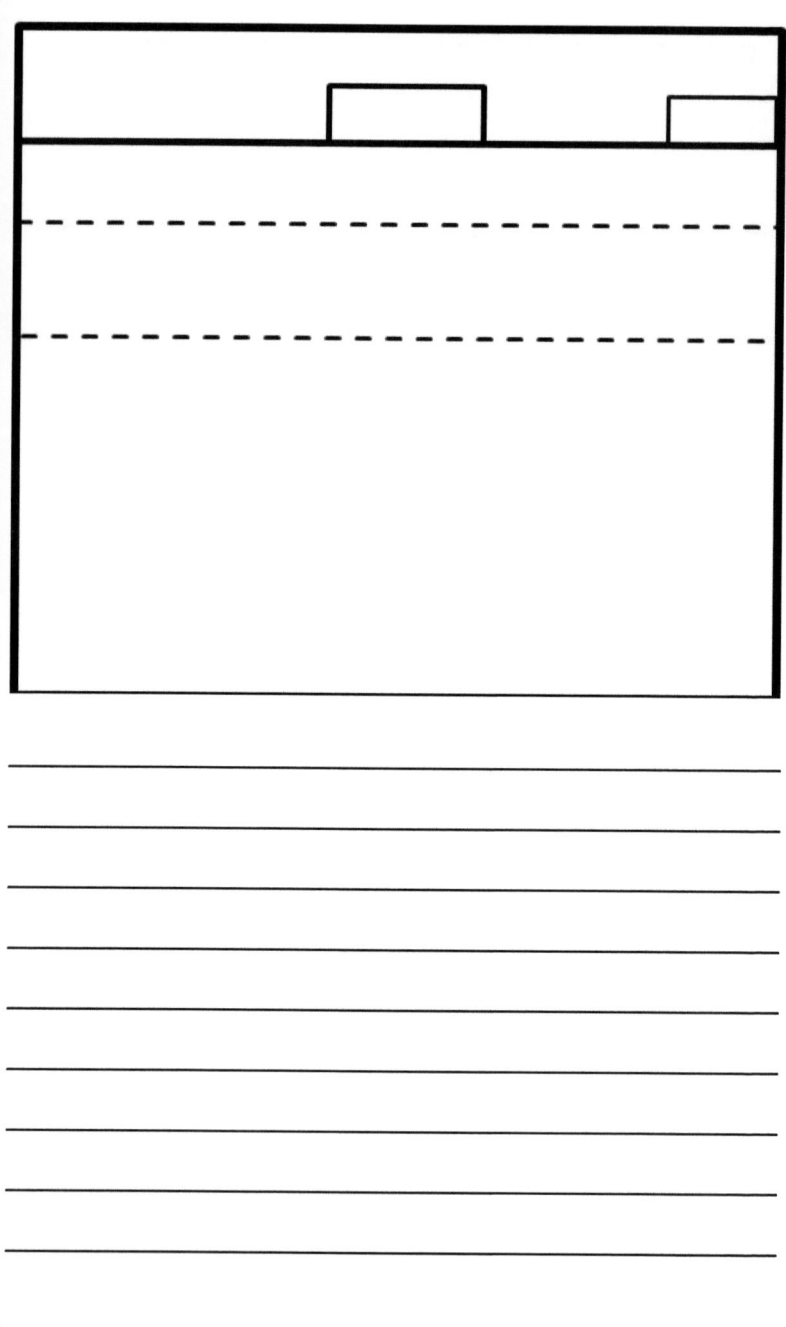

Theo von Taane

# Wasserball 2 in 1
# Taktikboard & Trainingsbuch

Das 2 in 1 Taktikboard & Trainingsbuch zur schnellen Erstellung von coaching Anweisungen/Spieltaktiken und -plänen, enthält nicht nur sportspezifische Vorlagen (Spielfeld und Raum für Notizen), sondern verfügt auch über eine wieder beschreibbare Fläche (Cover des Buchs), welche mit handelsüblichen whiteboard Stiften beschrieben werden kann und trocken abwischbar ist.

VORTEILE:
- Taktikbuch mit sportspezifischen Vordrucken (Spielfeld) zum schnellen und einfachen Skizzieren von Spieltaktiken/Übungen.
- Sind alle Seiten des Buches aufgebraucht, lässt sich das Cover unter Nutzung von whiteboard Stiften als Taktikboard unbegrenzt weiternutzen.
- Durch das handliche Format sowohl unterwegs als auch vor Ort zum Spiel oder Training nutzbar.
- Ideal zum spontanen Sammeln von Trainingsideen oder als Gedankenstütze.
- Ideal um dem Schüler durch schnelles Skizzieren der Übung den geplanten Trainingsablauf begreifbarer zu machen.
- Ideal zum Festhalten von geplante Spielzügen, um sie sich kurz vor dem Match oder währenddessen wieder ins Gedächtnis zu rufen.

*Bibliografische Information der Deutschen Nationalbibliothek:*
*Die Deutsche Nationalbibliothek verzeichnet diese Publikation in der Deutschen Nationalbibliografie; detaillierte bibliografische Daten sind im Internet über http://dnb.dnb.de abrufbar.*

© 2016 Theo von Taane; 1. Auflage

Texte und Illustrationen: **Theo von Taane**

Herstellung und Verlag: BoD – Books on Demand, Norderstedt

*ISBN: 9783739231440*

# Weitere Bücher von Theo von Taane

- Happy – Wünsch dir was! — ISBN: 9783734728570
- Tennis Witze Knallbonbons — ISBN: 9783732296490
- Tennis Postkarten Kalender — ISBN: 9783734741289
- Witze rund um Volleyball — ISBN: 9783734731801
- Witze rund um Basketball — ISBN: 9783734703824
- Witze rund ums Schwimmen — ISBN: 9783734734460
- Witze rund um Schach — ISBN: 9783734731658
- Witze rund um Tischtennis — ISBN: 9783734731648
- Witze rund um Eishockey — ISBN: 9783734730716
- Witze rund ums Fechten — ISBN: 9783734731976
- Witze rund um Handball — ISBN: 9783734731690
- Witze rund um Badminton — ISBN: 9783734732875
- Witze rund um Karate — ISBN: 9783734731666
- Witze rund um Judo — ISBN: 9783734731674
- Witze rund um Golf — ISBN: 9783734731704
- Witze rund um Fußball — ISBN: 9783734731712

u.s.w.

Von Theo von Taane gibt es auch viele Rätsel-, Witze- , Spiele-, Ausmal- und Notizbüche Bücher zum Thema MINECRAFT.

Des Weiteren bietet Theo von Taane Taktikboard und Trainingsbücher auch zu folgende Sportarten an:

- Badminton
- Baseball
- Basketball
- Bowling
- Cricket
- Eishockey
- Fechten
- Feldhockey
- Fußball
- Futsal
- Handball
- Lacrosse (w)
- Lacrosse (m)
- Netball
- Rugby
- Schach
- Squash
- Tennis
- Tischtennis
- Volleyball
- Wasserball

u.v.m.
Einfach nach ‚von Taane' im Webshop suchen um sich die mehr als 200 Theo von Taane Bücher anzeigen zu lassen.

# Books of Theo von Taane

| book | ISBN / order nr. |
|---|---|
| Football Tacticboard & Training Workbook | 9783734749605 |
| Badminton Tacticboard & Training Workbook | 9783734749643 |
| Baseball Tacticboard & Training Workbook | 9783734749650 |
| Basketball Tacticboard & Training Workbook | 9783734749681 |
| Bowling Tacticboard & Training Workbook | 9783734749698 |
| Cricket Tacticboard & Training Workbook | 9783734749711 |
| Ice Hockey Tacticboard & Training Workbook | 9783734749728 |
| Fencing Tacticboard & Training Workbook | 9783734749735 |
| Field Hockey Tacticboard & Training Workbook | 9783734749810 |
| Football (Soccer) Tacticboard & Training Workbook | 9783734749827 |
| Futsal Tacticboard & Training Workbook | 9783734749834 |
| Handball Tacticboard & Training Workbook | 9783734749841 |
| Lacrosse Women Tacticboard & Training Workbook | 9783734749858 |
| Lacrosse Men Tacticboard & Training Workbook | 9783734749865 |
| Netball Tacticboard & Training Workbook | 9783734749872 |
| Rugby Tacticboard & Training Workbook | 9783734749889 |
| Chess Tacticboard & Training Workbook | 9783734749896 |
| Squash Tacticboard & Training Workbook | 9783734749902 |
| Tennis Tacticboard & Training Workbook | 9783734749919 |
| Table Tennis Tacticboard & Training Workbook | 9783734749926 |
| Volleyball Tacticboard & Training Workbook | 9783734749933 |
| Water Polo Tacticboard & Training Workbook | 9783734749940 |

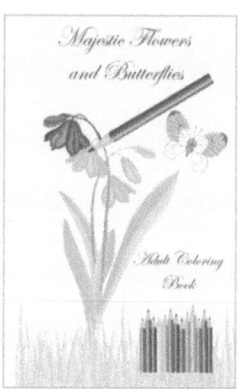

## Majestic Flowers and Butterflies
- Adult Coloring Book - ISBN: 9783739227085

This coloring book for adults contains 36 beautiful patterns of various flowers. Experience hours full of stress relief, mindful calm, creative expression and fun.

Use crayons, felt-tip pens and colored pencils to give the patterns a personal touch.

Millions of people worldwide have rediscovered the simple relaxation and joy of coloring!

Join this community and find yourself enchanted by the magical passion of inspiring coloring.